CONTENTS

INTRODUCTION

The graciousness of the Renaissance and the imposing styles of Neoclassical and Beaux Arts architecture have helped shape museums for centuries. Museum architecture has traditionally emphasized the ceremonial—resulting in grand staircases, columned porticos, soaring rotundas, and vaulted exhibition halls intended to awe the visitor with the importance of their content. In the twentieth century, the Modern movement in architecture turned from the ceremonial structure toward a more vernacular architecture, where museum buildings were seen as neutral, flexible containers, and designed accordingly. Current architects, though, have returned to the concept of the ceremonial structure. The museum has once again become a temple to art, in addition to being a work of art in its own right. And, as architects have freed themselves from the traditional design concepts of the museum, and worked to accommodate the changing social demands of these institutions, they have produced buildings that are masterpieces of creativity.

A Brief History of the Museum

The Greek word *mouseion* originally described ancient temples dedicated to the Muses, the patron goddesses of arts and sciences. Literary societies also held competitions at temples, so the term was broadened to include secular activities. The Greek philosopher Aristotle collected specimens from the natural world, which became part of the study and teaching facilities at his lyceum—one early type of museum. Another museum facility was created in the ancient Egyptian city of Alexandria by King Ptolemy I for the purpose of protecting precious texts and objects from political turmoil. The Alexandrian model was widely copied in succeeding centuries, though none of these ancient institutions has survived the test of time.

Renaissance interest in classical knowledge revived the memory of Alexandria's museum. However, during that period the word "museum" was used both for rooms containing collections of objects and for books describing collections. Other terms were used as well: Renaissance princes formed collections known as

OPPOSITE: The concept of the museum as a place for the general public to see and admire art developed slowly. The Medici and other aristocratic families opened their doors to a limited number of well-chosen viewers, but for a long time the wider public was excluded. Meanwhile, huge collections were being created, like those of the Vatican, seen here, in preparation for the time when the arts would be available to all.

ABOVE: Soon after the fall of the monarchy in the French Revolution, the Louvre was turned from a royal residence into an art museum. Here is a scene from this period of transition, *Project for the Disposition of the Grand Gallery, 1796* by Hubert Robert.

studioli, which grouped precious objects from ancient and contemporary periods together with natural history specimens. Scientific inquiries and voyages of discovery yielded jumbled collections of unrelated objects that became known as "cabinets of curiosity," or *Wunderkammern.* Paintings and sculpture collected by royalty, landed aristocracy, and the Church were displayed in *Kunstkammern* (art rooms).

The Renaissance saw the first buildings and rooms constructed specifically to highlight such art collections, as well as the first use of collections to underscore social prestige and power. In the eighteenth century, Enlightenment thinking inspired a movement toward allowing public access to art collections, as well as the beginnings of art history as an academic discipline. Scholars helped organize collections in a chronological manner stressing artistic development and separating national schools of artists. Connoisseurs, meanwhile, arranged art works based on aesthetic relationships, color, or subject. The architecture of the ideal museum was described for the first time, and included a central rotunda and vaulted galleries arranged symmetrically around four courtyards—a model that was seized upon by early museum architects. Ultimately, political upheaval, starting with the French Revolution and augmented by Napoleon's military campaigns, spurred the creation of national museums in France. Treasures poured in from Napoleon's conquests—and then back across Europe, when pillaged works were returned to their rightful owners after Napoleon's fall.

Museums were created to promote social unity, to educate and uplift the public, and to promote national pride—values that are still guiding principles in museums today. The aesthetics of display became ever more highly developed, and "period rooms," intended to give visitors a total experience of a moment in history, became very popular. One early and influential public art gallery, the Dulwich Picture Gallery in London, alternated square and rectangular rooms that were lit from above, a model that was widely imitated.

Economic growth in the United States concentrated wealth in the hands of a few industrialists and financiers who had the means and influence to found art museums in many American cities. The end of the nineteenth century saw an increase in other types of museums, as well, with a focus on natural history, industry, and history. Expositions with many types of objects displayed together in large pavilions also stimulated new ideas about display.

The twentieth century, which has seen a proliferation of museums throughout the world, has also brought new questions about what a museum building should be. Early twentieth-century museums were imposing monuments that celebrated their treasures architecturally. After 1940, there was a trend toward museums which provided a neutral, universal space, or alternatively, the museum was itself intended as a sculptural work of art.

Today, new demands are being made on the museum building as it evolves into a popular entertainment center that also educates, feeds, merchandises, providing a social as well as a spiritual experience. Additionally, many museums now have Internet websites which are becoming increasingly comprehensive as the international on-line audience expands. Museum websites not only make exhibitions and collections widely accessible, they also encourage displays of art created expressly for digital media. Already, museums are able to bring their missions to millions of virtual visitors, and although the Internet cannot duplicate the experience of seeing actual works of art, it offers a powerful alternative to the traditional museum visit. Ultimately, though, the shape of future museums will continue to evolve according to current social needs.

FOLLOWING PAGE: The glass pyramid at the Louvre is seen here illuminated and surrounded by a glass roof that provides daylight for public areas located beneath the main plaza area. Though controversial at the outset, the Louvre pyramid has come to symbolize the dynamic forward–looking spirit of the arts in France.

CHAPTER ONE

RENAISSANCE AND NEOCLASSICAL MUSEUMS

The idea of the museum came of age in Renaissance Italy. Private art collections, such as those of the influential Florentine family, the Medici, as well as the art treasures of the Vatican in Rome, formed the nucleus of great collections. The architectural style of the Renaissance, which refined and codified the achievements of ancient Roman architecture, also formed the basis for the style of the buildings housing the collections. These museums, which include the Uffizi, the Pitti Palace, and the Vatican Museums, today retain an amazing historical continuity in which to display the treasures of this period known for a rebirth and flowering of the arts.

The Bargello

The National Museum of the Bargello in Florence, which houses a magnificent collection of Florentine Renaissance sculpture, as well as bronzes and decorative arts, is actually a medieval building constructed in 1255 as a city hall. In 1261, this rugged masonry structure, with its highly fortified towers, became the official residence of the "Podestà," the governing magistrate of the city. Its castle-like appearance is a reminder of the hazards of political life in medieval Florence. From 1575 the building served as police headquarters and it became known as the "Bargello" after the title of its chief police officer. Much of the building was converted to prison cells; the courtyard, now a lovely display area for sculpture, held a scaffold for public executions. In the mid-nineteenth century, the provincial government of Tuscany decided that the Bargello should become a museum; the prison was dismantled and the building restored. So it was that the Bargello, which now houses some 30,000 decorative works, became Italy's first national museum.

The Uffizi

When the center of government moved from the Bargello to the Palazzo Vecchio, Duke Cosimo I de' Medici decided to build the Uffizi Palace to serve as the Florentine state's administrative center. In 1560, Cosimo I commissioned Giorgio Vasari to build the Uffizi. The Uffizi was Vasari's masterpiece, striking in perspective, with two long parallel structures framing a courtyard, joined at the end where the foundations are almost resting over the River Arno. Construction took twenty years, and the building was completed by Bernardo

ABOVE: The Tribune, an octagonal room in the Uffizi created by Bernardo Buontalenti, attracts visitors from all over the world, just as it did when it was new. It is top–lit, allowing ample wall space for displaying art. This room would have important influence on future museum design.

LEFT: The imposing bell tower of the Uffizi Palace proclaims the importance of this Medici structure as both a center of power and as the cultural center of Florence. The Uffizi was the first museum to allow visits from outsiders, although on a very limited basis.

Buontalenti after Vasari's death in 1574, the same year that Cosimo I died.

Francesco I, Cosimo I's son, succeeded his father in shaping the destiny of the Uffizi. Francesco I's interest in science, alchemy, and art led him to dedicate the second floor of the Uffizi to his private interests. In the west wing he set up laboratories for the creation of medicines, perfumes, poisons, and antidotes, while the top of the east wing was devoted to the family collection of ancient sculpture and artworks. Buontalenti created a special octagonal room, known as the Tribune, which was top–lit to allow maximum display space on the walls, and contained a special cabinet for exhibiting smaller curiosities. Considered to be a superb example of Late Renaissance or Mannerist architecture, the Uffizi embodies the classic design principals of harmony, balance, and coherence. The Tribune Room, in particular, soon became a famous destination, attracting visitors from all over Europe, and had an important impact on the nascent discipline of museum architecture.

By housing the Medici art collections in a central place near the heart of the city, Florence also made them a symbol of its cultural prestige—a precedent which is still at work in city planning today. From the beginning, the museum was encyclopedic and universal in nature, well in keeping with the humanistic spirit of the times. The Medici family continued to add to the collections right up until 1737, when their line died out, and they ensured by decree that city treasures could not be removed if the political fortunes of the city changed. They also were the first rulers, by several centuries, to allow the museum to be visited on request—although only by people of high rank.

Today, thanks to the Medici, the Uffizi contains the greatest collection of Florentine painting in the world, and it can be enjoyed in a genuine Renaissance setting, together with superb views of the river and city. Above the galleries, a secret corridor connects all the important elements of Francisco I's political center, from the Uffizi and the Palazzo Vecchio to the Pitti Palace, which was the Medici family residence after 1550.

ABOVE: The Uffizi Palace in Florence, commissioned in 1560, is the work of Giorgio Vasari and Bernardo Buontalenti. The Renaissance fascination with perspective is apparent here, where two long colonnaded structures recede into the distance, drawing the eye toward the River Arno.

RIGHT: Galleries, such as this one in the Uffizi Palace, were created especially to display the artworks of the Medici collection. Because of the Medici family's passion for collecting, the Uffizi houses today the greatest collection of Florentine painting in the world, as well as masterpieces from other schools of art.

The Pitti Palace

Florence's Pitti Palace, which now houses the Palatine Gallery, the Gallery of Modern Art, and the Museum of Silver, was commissioned by Luca Pitti, a chief magistrate of the Florentine Republic who wanted to outdo the Medici. However, the Pitti merchants were outmaneuvered by the Medici's wealth and power and, in 1549, the palace was sold to Cosimo I. Begun about 1457, the Pitti's design is attributed to architect and sculptor Filippo Brunelleschi, who is regarded as the father of Renaissance architecture. One of Florence's largest palaces, the Pitti adjoins the beautiful Boboli Gardens—an authentic Renaissance garden commissioned by Cosimo I. The plan of the Pitti Palace is grouped around three internal courtyards and a huge open forecourt. The severe façade of heavily rusticated stone is arranged on horizontal lines with moldings and simple friezes dividing the stories. The roof is topped by a strong cornice. Although the exterior is almost unadorned, the interior courts are graced by colonnades and the rooms are luxuriously appointed. The collections contain more than 500 masterpieces by the greatest artists of the sixteenth and seventeenth centuries, as well as treasure–troves of silver, gems, ivory, porcelain, and glass.

LEFT: The design of the Pitti Palace in Florence is attributed to the early Renaissance architect Filippo Brunelleschi, who is best known for his design for the dome of Florence's great cathedral. The rough exterior gives no indication of the lavishly decorated rooms to be found within.

LEFT: Almost as remarkable as the superb artworks on view at the Pitti Palace is the splendor of the building's interior design. This gallery, with its magnificently embellished vaulted ceiling, is a sampling of the many wonders to be found in all parts of the palace.

LEFT: The galleries of the Pitti Palace are perfect for the display of great masterpieces, of which many from the sixteenth and seventeenth centuries can be found in the museum's collection. The Pitti Palace houses the Palatine Gallery, the Gallery of Modern Art, and the Museum of Silver.

The Vatican Museums

The Roman Catholic Church was another powerful patron and collector of the arts in Italy. Indeed, the Church's interests overlapped with those of the Medici family, who produced three popes and several Roman Catholic cardinals. The Church had also, in one sense, functioned as an early type of museum, displaying religious works of art on its walls and in its treasuries—reliquaries, liturgical vessels, crosses, and bejeweled missals. The fabulous collections housed in the Vatican Museums include antiquities from ancient Egypt, Greece, and Rome and some of the world's most famous sculpture, such as the *Apollo Belvedere* and the *Laocoön*. Private rooms of the main palaces built by Renaissance popes were decorated by Raphael Sanzio, and the famed ceiling of the Sistine Chapel was frescoed by Michelangelo Buonarroti.

The Vatican collections are housed in a number of different buildings. These include the first art museum expressly built for that purpose—the Pio Clementine Museum, which was begun in 1770 and constructed in stages following the designs

BELOW: Vatican City in Rome boasts a complex of museums filled with treasures accumulated over centuries. The Pio Clementine Museum, dating from 1770, is the centerpiece and is surrounded by the Chiaramonti Museum, the Egyptian Museum, the Etruscan Museum, and the Braccio Nuovo.

RIGHT: *Laocoön*, one of a handful of great masterpieces surviving from antiquity, is a highlight of the Vatican Museums' collections. The sculpture vividly depicts the death agony of the Trojan priest Laocoön and his two sons, as they are attacked by sea serpents before the walls of Troy.

LEFT: Visiting the Vatican Museums is truly a journey into the past. Objects of every kind, from every period of history are on display in magnificently designed and decorated rooms and galleries that are in themselves works of art.

of architects Alessandro Dori, Michelangelo Simonetti, and Guiseppe Camporese. The design of this museum incorporated features that would become standard in future museums for many years: a grand staircase, a domed rotunda (resembling the Pantheon), an open courtyard, and long galleries with majestic vaults. The Vatican Museums—including the Pio Clementine Museum; the Chiaramonti Museum (1807–10); the Egyptian Museum and the Etruscan Museum (1837–39); and the Braccio Nuovo (1817–22)—were all built in the age of Neoclassicism.

Neoclassical Temples

Neoclassicism succeeded the Rococo style in the second half of the eighteenth century. This age saw the construction of the first true public museums. Architects blended the formal vocabulary of Greek and Roman architecture with Renaissance spatial concepts. The resulting marriage of Greek and Roman structural systems of colonnades, vaults, and domes, with the Renaissance grace of cabinets, galleries, and courtyards, became the archetype of the public museum. Since the collections of the first museums centered on the art of ancient

ABOVE: Among the many achievements of the great Renaissance artist Raphael are the decorations of the papal apartments—entire rooms filled with lively, colorful frescoes of extraordinary freshness and vitality. For a man who lived only thirty–seven years, he left behind an enormous body of work.

Greece and Rome, and of the Renaissance, the buildings were a perfect compliment to their contents.

Museum Island

The five museums of Museum Island in Berlin might be mistaken for a collection of classical temples perched on an island in the Spree River. The Old Museum was built first (1823–30); its architect, Karl Friedrich Schinkel, set the course for the complimentary designs of the New Museum (1843–50), the Old National Gallery (1866–76), the Bode Museum (1897–1904), and the Pergamon Museum (1933). The idea of a public museum to uplift the middle classes by exposing them to art was developed in Berlin by the archaeologist Aloys Hirt, who was Schinkel's professor. However, Napoleon's conquest of Prussia in 1806 and the subsequent removal of many art treasures to the Imperial Museum in the Louvre delayed implementation of this popular plan. When the artworks were repatriated and returned to display after Napoleon's fall, the king approved the idea of a museum to be built facing the royal residence, and the decorative program of the building was to pay special homage to him through inscriptions and statuary.

Schinkel's Old Museum has a façade formed of a long colonnade of 40–foot high (12 meters) Ionic columns. The building

ABOVE: Museum Island in Berlin is home to a complex of five museums that house artworks of the highest quality and distinction. Built over the course of one hundred years on an island in the Spree River, these structures were severely damaged by bombing raids during World War II. Though one of these has been restored, the others will reopen in the next few years.

is entered by means of a monumental double staircase leading up into the colonnade and a concealed second level. The front of the building is of stone, for a grand effect, but the rest of the building is made of brick, the most readily available regional building material at the time. The foundation presented its builders with a challenge—a complicated system of wooden pilings was driven into the swampy bog of the island. Schinkel set out to create a building that would be a cross between a castle, a church, and the ideal museum of the time. The building was intended to produce a feeling of exaltation, the domed Pantheon–like hall was to be a sanctuary for treasures, and the vast murals behind the colonnade depicted a grand vision of the place of art within civilization.

Museum Island houses a rich collection of art treasures that represent only part of Berlin's substantial art holdings. The buildings were severely damaged during World War II, but the art survived—hidden in numerous underground repositories. When the Berlin Wall was built, Museum Island continued to draw tourists, and many made the border crossing from West to East to view the museum collections which include many famous architectural antiquities, among them the Pergamon Altar (a monumental Greek temple dating from 180 BC) and the Ishtar Gate of Babylon. After the reunification of East and West Germany, much controversy surrounded plans for Museum Island. The Old Museum finally reopened after renovations in 1998. The Old National Gallery, with its outstanding collection of eighteenth–through early twentieth–century paintings and sculpture, is scheduled to reopen around 2000, and the New Museum, still undergoing renovation and reconstruction, will follow.

The British Museum

Another great Neoclassical "temple" is the British Museum in London, which began as the private collection of Sir Hans Sloane and the library of Sir Robert Cotton. Founded in 1753, it was the first museum in Europe specifically intended to be open to the public, although in reality access was severely limited. Priceless treasures flowed in from all corners of the British Empire so that it now possesses a world–famous collection of antiquities from Egypt, Western Asia, Greece and Rome, as well as prehistoric, Romano–British, Medieval, Renaissance, modern, and Oriental collections comprising some six–and–a–half million objects. Among them are such landmarks of western civilization as the Elgin Marbles, the Rosetta Stone, and the *Gutenberg Bible.*

ABOVE: The Elgin Marbles are among the most important objects in the British Museum. They are fragments of statues by Phidias that once adorned the pediment of the Parthenon in ancient Athens. Though their acquisition in the early nineteenth century was not questioned at the time, their retention by the museum is a matter of controversy between the Greek and British governments.

RIGHT: Aided by the enormous power and reach of the British Empire during the nineteenth century, the British Museum was able to acquire considerable holdings of artworks and cultural objects representing an array of periods and cultures from around the world.

Room
20

RIGHT: The imposing structure housing the collections of the British Museum was designed by Sir Robert Smirke in 1823 and finally completed and opened to the public in 1848. This world famous building has influenced the design and planning of many other museums.

BELOW: The National Gallery in London was conceived as a temple for the arts. Therefore, it was fitting that its architect William Wilkins—an avid enthusiast of the Greek Revival style—should be chosen to design this graceful Neoclassical structure.

The British Museum was housed in a number of different buildings before it settled into its present Greek Revival quarters. The 1823 design by Sir Robert Smirke, an architect who was a leader in that movement, was finally completed in 1848. The British Museum has a massive Palladian façade, numerous Ionic columns, pedimental sculptures, and lofty exhibition halls that have influenced museum architecture world wide since their creation. The Great Court at the heart of the Museum houses the famous Reading Room, and is currently being transformed by the architects Foster and Partners into a two–acre public square enclosed by a spectacular glass roof. The departure of the British Library to its own building has freed space for a new center for education, temporary exhibition galleries, and other facilities, while the Reading Room rotunda will reopen as an open–access reference library and the courtyard will once again become the focus of the building, as originally intended.

The National Gallery

When London's National Gallery was established in 1824, the English architect William Wilkins won the competition for its design. Wilkins, a promoter of the Greek Revival style, wanted to erect a temple of the arts that would enshrine and present for public enjoyment and study an outstanding group of paintings whose nucleus was assembled by philanthropist and collector John Julius Angerstein. The museum, with its Neoclassical portico graced by tall Ionic columns, was completed in 1838, and is situated on London's Trafalgar Square. The most recent and ambitious addition to the National Gallery was the 1991 Sainsbury Wing, designed by the American architects Robert Venturi and Denise Scott Brown to house the institution's early Renaissance collection. The new galleries were intended to evoke the feeling of a fifteenth–century Tuscan palace, even to the use of *pietra serena*, a gray Florentine stone also used for the Uffizi.

The Prado

Madrid's Prado opened to the public in 1819, when King Ferdinand VII's painting collections were installed in an imposing Neoclassical building created by Spanish architect Juan de Villanueva. The building was originally commissioned in 1785 as a gallery of natural sciences and arts by Charles III, but never used for that purpose. Instead, it was completed and renovated to house the royal collections for

LEFT: As visitors approach the rotunda entrance to the Prado's main gallery, they are confronted by a bronze statue of one of Spain's great leaders, King Charles I. The victorious figure seen here eventually became Holy Roman Emperor Charles V and raised Spain to the status of a dominant European power.

FOLLOWING PAGE: This view of the Reading Room of the British Museum, though recently made, is now a part of history. Like other areas of the museum, it is being remodeled and will soon reopen as an open–access reference library.

RIGHT: Two classical statues flank the entrance to a gallery in the Prado Museum that contains one of the great treasures of Spanish painting, *The Family of Charles IV* by Francisco de Goya. Founded originally as a natural science museum, the Prado later amassed huge holdings of Spanish art, augmented by the works of major artists from many other countries and periods.

public enjoyment, conservation, and research. Today, the Prado contains masterpieces by Spain's greatest painters, including Francisco Goya, Diego Velázquez, and El Greco, as well as Flemish and Italian works.

De Villanueva's building has classical façades, with Doric columns on its great western porch and Ionic columns on the northern loggias. The rectangular plan and two–storied elevation, with soaring galleries and rotundas, follows the classic model, while the building materials are regional, from the open brickwork to the decorations of local granite and limestone. When Ferdinand VII decided to use the building as a picture gallery, it had suffered from use as a storehouse for military equipment during the French invasion. Funds were allocated not only for restoration, but also to complete the sculptural decorations of the façade, which included allegorical statues and medallions of the great Spanish artists. In 1998, the Prado once again underwent renovation, including the installation of a new roof, the addition of temporary galleries and restoration studios, and other much needed services.

RIGHT: A statue of the Spanish master Diego Velázquez sits, brooding, before the Prado Museum in Madrid. This elegant Neoclassical building was begun by Juan de Villanueva in 1785. However, because of the vagaries of politics and the outbreak of continental war, it was not completed and opened until more than thirty years later.

LEFT: Though the Prado in Madrid was opened in 1819, it was been renovated and up–dated many times. This view of the museum's Rubens gallery shows how well the modern blending of fine materials and simple design can enhance the display of great art.

The Hermitage

The State Hermitage Museum in St. Petersburg reflects the taste, wealth, and passion for art collecting of Catherine the Great, who ruled Russia from 1762 to 1796. The Hermitage is housed in five buildings representing many styles of architecture, from Russian Baroque to Neoclassical and Neo–Renaissance. The museum was founded in 1764, when Catherine purchased a collection of 225 paintings, although it was not formally opened to the public until 1852. Construction soon began on the Small Hermitage by architects Vallin de la Mothe and Yuri Felten, which was to be used by Catherine as a museum and a private retreat from court. In 1787, Felten began a new building, the Old Hermitage, to house the growing royal collections. A Neoclassical addition with Greek motifs, the New Hermitage was completed in 1851 by German architect Leo von Klenze on commission from Nicholas I.

The Winter Palace, which had served as the residence of Russia's rulers from Catherine the Great to Nicholas II, was added to the Hermitage buildings following the fall of the Imperial government in the October Revolution of 1917.

LEFT: The grand staircase of the Hermitage, the former Winter Palace in St. Petersburg, is a triumph of the Russian Baroque style. The extravagant juxtaposition of exuberant frieze work and carvings with accents of malachite and gold is typical of the Russian manner.

ABOVE: The Hermitage, the former Winter Palace in St. Petersburg, sits on Palace Square facing the Alexander Column, a monument celebrating Russia's defeat of Napoleon in 1812. Though a royal residence from 1762 to 1917, the museum portion of the building, containing the vast imperial collection, was opened to the public in 1852

RIGHT: The statuary hall of the Hermitage is one of many galleries that displays the richness and depth of the museum's collection. Apart from masterpieces of European painting from the Middle Ages to the present, there is also on view the art of India, China, Egypt, Greece, and Rome.

Created by the Italian architect Bartolomeo Francesco Rastrelli and completed in 1762, the Winter Palace is built in the ornate Russian Baroque style, with highly–decorated windows and a roof balustrade topped with statues and vases. The museum buildings have remained relatively untouched, so that today the Hermitage still maintains the character of a mid–nineteenth–century palace–museum. The Hermitage has one of the most impressive international art collections anywhere, including French, Italian, and Spanish masters, Impressionist masterpieces, Egyptian antiquities, and Russian icons, as well as jewels, gold, and precious objects. Currently short of funds following the collapse of the Soviet Union, the Hermitage is reaching out to the international community for assistance in maintaining its collections.

LEFT: Soon after the Russian Revolution, the Hermitage—the court museum of the tsars—was joined with the former imperial residence to become a single giant museum. Not only can visitors see one of the greatest collections of art in the world, but they can enjoy a wealth of architectural and decorative creations.

RIGHT: The original Hermitage, as conceived by Catherine the Great, was an intimate, informal retreat, featuring artworks presented in beautiful surroundings. This small alcove in the former Winter Palace, with its many-hued marble inlays, is reminiscent of Catherine's wish to create small–scale settings amid the pomp of court life.

RIGHT: The new entrance to the Louvre provides a fresh, exciting approach to one of the world's great museums, creating an air of excitement and anticipation. Located just below the glass pyramid, this area features a museum shop, restaurant, and cafe for the public.

ABOVE: The contrast of old and new, classic and modern, is apparent here in this view of the Louvre—dating from the sixteenth century—and the late–twentieth century pyramid before it, created by I. M. Pei. Proving that fine design matches fine design, these two dissimilar structures appear quite harmonious.

The Louvre

Now the foremost French art museum, the Louvre in Paris was originally built as a fortress by Philip II in the late twelfth century. Today's Louvre began to take shape in 1546, when the art– and pleasure–loving king, Francis I, commissioned architect Pierre Lescot to build a new structure on the site. Then in 1564, Queen Catherine de' Medici commissioned architect Philibert Delorme to build a residence at the Tuileries and to connect it to the Louvre with a long gallery. The original buildings were enlarged and enhanced according to Neoclassical and traditional French designs under successive generations of rulers and architects. In 1791, Revolutionary leaders occupied the palace and a very busy guillotine faced the main entrance. The year 1793 saw the creation by decree of the *Musée Central des Arts* and the opening to the public of the *Grande Galerie* of the Louvre. During Napoleon I's reign, the museum was proclaimed the *Musée Napoléon,* and accumulated art from all over the Empire, most of which was returned after Napoleon's defeat. The grand architectural scheme of the Louvre was completed by Napoleon III during the Second Empire.

A series of renovations and additions undertaken in the late twentieth century include the glass Pyramid designed by

ABOVE: This painting shows the Louvre as it appeared in the mid–nineteenth century when the building's use as a museum had become firmly established. The Louvre had been expanded and enhanced many times over the years, but it was at the time of this painting that it achieved its present form under Napoleon III.

BELOW: The Alte Pinakothek in Munich is one of Germany's finest museums, taking much of its inspiration from Italian Renaissance architecture and from the Renaissance painter, Raphael. It also boasts fine modern galleries that are spacious enough to properly display large, bold works of art.

American architect I.M. Pei, which created a new focal point and entrance in the courtyard and tops a large museum shop, café, and restaurant. Also recently completed and restored as museum galleries is the entire Richelieu Wing, which was built as government offices in 1852–57, and had been home to the Finance Ministry since 1871. The Louvre's collections are vast—among them are many Greek, Roman, and Egyptian antiquities, and superb Old Master paintings including Leonardo da Vinci's *Mona Lisa*, and sculptures such as the *Venus of Milo* and the *Winged Victory of Samothrace*.

The Alte Pinakothek

Although it resembles a Neo–Renaissance palace, German architect Leo von Klenze's Alte Pinakothek in Munich was actually planned as a picture gallery. Completed in 1836, it was inspired by two specific Italian Renaissance buildings. Von Klenze, a master of eclectic architecture, was encouraged to experiment with Greek, Byzantine, and Renaissance styles by his royal patron, King Ludwig I. Von Klenze's historicism led him to believe that the whole architectural achievement of the past was available as inspiration for his buildings, and he drew on it readily. The Alte Pinakothek's interior decorative program is devoted to the painter, Raphael, and the cornerstone of the building was laid on his birthday. The statues on the top balustrade of the building depict the artists most admired at the time of its creation.

LEFT: Here is seen the exterior of the Neue Pinkothek in Munich. Its sleek, clean lines and surfaces are a sharp contrast to the ornamented, eclectic style of its older cousin, with its influences from Greek, Byzantine, and Renaissance sources.

RIGHT: Here is seen the *Galerie Percier* in the Louvre with its columned arches luring the visitor forward. Though the Louvre has been reshaped and changed over the centuries, much of its architectural style is Neoclasssical.

CHAPTER TWO

NINETEENTH—CENTURY STYLES

Beaux Arts is the term given to a flamboyant type of classical architecture popular in France and the United States during the nineteenth and early twentieth centuries. Education at the Parisian *Ecole des Beaux–Arts*, which became common for American as well as French architects, led to a style of building characterized by formal planning and rich decoration. At its most spectacular in large public structures, Beaux–Arts style is often recognizable by giant coupled columns, marked wall projections, groups of sculptured figures, and high–relief decorations such as swags, garlands, and medallions.

The Metropolitan Museum of Art

The face that The Metropolitan Museum of Art presents to New York's Fifth Avenue is classic Beaux Arts. The soaring columns and massive, jutting roofline are architectural proclamations that this is one of America's great cultural institutions. Richard Morris Hunt, the first American trained at the *Ecole des Beaux–Arts*, created this limestone façade as part of a master plan for the museum that expanded the structure around the original red brick Gothic Revival building designed by architects Calvert Vaux and Jacob Wrey Mould in 1874. Hunt's façade is flanked at either end with complimentary wings created by the architectural firm McKim, Mead and White. With great foresight in city planning, the Central Park location was selected at a time when that area of Manhattan was sparsely settled, allowing ample space for the museum to expand. And it has certainly

ABOVE: The façade of New York's Metropolitan Museum of Art is a perfect example of the Beaux–Arts style, a type of classical architecture that came to the fore in the late–nineteenth and early–twentieth centuries, particularly in France and the United States.

LEFT: The Great Hall of the Metropolitan Museum of Art was created by Richard Morris Hunt, who was also responsible for designing the museum's façade. This vast space, with its domes and soaring arches, welcomes millions of museum–goers every year, and also serves as a venue for gala celebrations.

FOLLOWING PAGE: The Philadelphia Museum of Art, atop a hill in the heart of the city, is a well–known and beloved landmark. Known to millions through the Sylvester Stallone film, *Rocky,* in which it symbolizes the pinnacle of achievement, this fine Neoclassical structure houses a great collection and is—as it seems—a temple of the arts.

RIGHT: Since the Metropolitan Museum's collection covers the art of many cultures and periods, its galleries are varied and have been carefully planned to house and display to full advantage the artworks for which they were designed. The gallery shown here is devoted to eighteenth– and nineteenth–century American art.

BELOW: The Metropolitan Museum's Armor Hall is a magnet for children of all ages. Here, full suits of armor of every type are displayed along with a comprehensive collection of weaponry from the past. This evocative, romantic installation fully evokes the Age of Chivalry.

continued to expand, thrusting wing after new wing into the park as its spectacularly rich collections have grown.

Since 1970, the architectural firm Kevin Roche John Dinkeloo and Associates has been overseeing the museum's expansion. The monumental front staircase, the glass pyramid of the Lehman wing, and the great glass–roofed courtyard of the American wing are only a few of their contributions. The firm has also restored Hunt's Great Hall, which, with its soaring vaults and domes, is considered one of the great spaces in New York City. Since ground was first broken for The Metropolitan Museum of Art, over a dozen architectural firms have worked on its design, and five master plans have been approved, representing more than a century of architectural history. The museum's holdings are truly encyclopedic, encompassing splendid collections of antiquities and fine arts from all over the world, and paintings and objects from literally every period and style.

RIGHT: The American Wing of the Metropolitan Museum of Art is one of the museum's most visited areas, where a rich collection of sculpture, painting, furniture, and decorative objects from America's past is one view. Monumental sculptures and architectural elements can be found in the wing's glass–enclosed atrium, seen here.

The Art Institute of Chicago

The original 1893 Beaux–Arts building of the Art Institute of Chicago also conveyed the idealism and cultural ambitions of that city. As with many American museums, its architecture preceded the collections it was meant to house. In fulfilling its mission to become a world–class art museum, the Art Institute has also seen more than a century of almost continual building, though fortunately, its now central site was chosen to accommodate these expansions. Originally part of Chicago's World's Columbian Exposition of 1893, the Art Institute was built on landfill bordering railroad tracks. Unlike most of the temporary Exposition buildings, the Art Institute was planned as a permanent limestone structure. Designed by the Boston architectural firm of Shepley, Rutan and Coolidge, it was occupied for a time by the World's Congress Auxiliary of the World's Columbian Exposition, and then turned over to the Art Institute to house both its museum and art school. Today this original building, which has strong Renaissance elements, is the face that greets visitors. Flanking the front steps are a pair of much–loved bronze lions by the American sculptor Edward L. Kemeys, which have come to symbolize the city of Chicago.

The Kunsthistoriches Museum

Vienna's Kunsthistoriches Museum ("Museum of Art History," in English) is also a monumental architectural symbol of its city's cultural pride. Part of an extensive program that saw the construction of many other important museum buildings in

BELOW: *The Assumption of the Virgin* by El Greco on view in the Art Institute of Chicago. Unlike the great museums of Europe, American museum collections were not built over the course of centuries. In fact, most of them have been amassed only within the last hundred years through the generosity of donors and art patrons.

Vienna at this time, this massive Beaux–Arts structure with Renaissance overtones was opened in 1891. Designed by architects Gottfried von Semper and Karl Hasenauer, the Kunsthistoriches Museum is an elegant stone amalgam of columns, statuary, and domes. The focus of the building is a grand staircase adorned with monumental sculpture and

RIGHT: The Art Institute of Chicago was built in 1893 as part of the World's Columbian Exposition of that year. Built in the Beaux–Arts, style it was first used to house exhibits. At the conclusion of the Exposition, it was occupied by the Art Institute and soon became one of America's most prominent museums.

LEFT: One of the glories of Vienna is the Kunsthistoriches Museum, or Art History Museum, which first opened in 1891. This impressive Beaux–Arts structure was designed by Gottfried von Semper—architect of the renowned Dresden Opera House—and Karl Hasenauer.

decorated by Viennese artists. There is also a domed octagonal room that recalls the Uffizi's Tribune, and testifies to the strong continuity in museum architecture stretching forward from the Renaissance. The collections of this world–famous museum were amassed by the Hapsburg family, the ruling house of Austria from 1282 to 1918.

The Pennsylvania Academy of the Fine Arts

During the last quarter of the nineteenth century, Eclecticism in architecture was widely practiced and accepted, and architects drew elements from different styles of the past, combining them with the latest building techniques. The popular Victorian Gothic movement partook of this historicism as well, using the decorative and structural forms of medieval Gothic architecture to give sentiment and depth to modern architecture. The innovative American architect Frank Furness produced a highly original and eclectic Victorian Gothic building for the Pennsylvania Academy of the Fine Arts, which opened in Philadelphia in 1876. Founded in 1805 as a combination museum and art school, the Pennsylvania Academy had outgrown two previous Neoclassical buildings before Furness won the competition to produce its new quarters. Furness' façade is a true mixture of styles, combining a Greek sculptured frieze, a French mansard roof, Renaissance rusticated stone, Gothic arches and tracery, medieval corbels, and Native American rug patterns. The total exterior effect is that of multicolored jewel–box splendor, reinforced when ascending the grand staircase into a four–story Gothic–arched hall flooded with natural light and brilliant colors. Red walls are studded with gold rosettes, and ceiling vaults resemble a blue sky with silver stars. The rotunda is adorned with gilded, polychromed iron columns. The entire building was lovingly restored in 1976 and displays a chronologically–arranged collection of the finest examples of American art from the 1760s to the present.

LEFT: Frank Furness designed the highly original Pennsylvania Academy of Fine Arts which opened in 1876. The eclectic style he employed—Victorian Gothic—is clearly seen here in this view of the Academy's grand staircase.

RIGHT: Standing at the core of Vienna's Kunsthistorische Museum is this breathtaking grand staircase. Monumental statuary and the creation of design and pattern through the use of many–hued marbles make this a unique public space.

The Isabella Stewart Gardner Museum

Fantasy also defines the architecture of Boston's beloved Isabella Stewart Gardner Museum. Originally called Fenway Court, the museum was built according to the vision of its namesake and founder in the style of a fifteenth—century Venetian palace, with the assistance of architect and engineer Willard T. Sears. Opened in 1903, it was designed both as a private residence for Mrs. Gardner, and as a museum for her collection of Italian Renaissance and seventeenth—century Dutch masterpieces, many of which she acquired on the advice of noted art historian Bernard Berenson.

Focused inward, away from the preying eyes of Boston society, the heart of the museum is centered on a gracious glass—roofed courtyard. This flower—filled sculpture garden often serves as the setting for chamber music concerts. Opening into the courtyard are three floors of graceful Venetian balconies with arched Gothic windows and delicate tracery. Mrs. Gardner had very specific ideas not only about the architecture of her museum, but also about the display of her collections. She grouped objects according to her own ideas, and avoided labels, wishing for visitors to have an aesthetic rather than an educational experience. She lived on the fourth

ABOVE: The Gardner Museum, designed by William T. Sears, was originally known as Fenway Court. It was designed in the style of a fifteenth—century Venetian palace with its charming balconies and Gothic windows.

BELOW: The collection of the Gardner Museum centers on works of the Italian Renaissance and the paintings of the seventeenth—century Dutch masters. Although no work in the museum may be sold, the collection has unfortunately been diminished in recent years by the theft of several important paintings.

ABOVE: The artworks in the galleries of the Isabella Stewart Gardner Museum are arranged, unlabeled, according to the express wishes of Mrs. Gardner herself. This arrangement can never be altered.

LEFT: The heart of the Isabella Stewart Gardner Museum in Boston is the glass—roofed courtyard and sculpture garden. The museum was built in 1903 by Mrs. Gardner, and originally intended as both private residence for herself and a museum for her collection.

RIGHT: Here Rembrandt's well–known *Night Watch* is on view in a gallery of the Rijksmuseum. The museum's collection is especially strong in the paintings of Dutch artists from the fifteen to eighteenth centuries. Out of all of them, of course, Rembrandt is the star attraction.

BELOW: This detail from the façade of the Rikjsmuseum shows Cuypers interest in the use of colored bricks and other elements to enrich the exterior texture of his buildings. Here is shown a frieze depicting a group of Dutch burghers silhouetted against a brightly colored background.

floor until her death in 1924, with the museum open to the public on selected days, and often used for her private artistic and musical salons. According to the terms of her will, the arrangement of the collection can never be altered, and nothing may be sold or added—assuring the survival of this unique institution.

The Rijksmuseum

An eclectic mixture of architectural styles is also united in the Neo–Gothic building designed by P.J.H. Cuypers to house the Rijksmuseum in Amsterdam. The building, which opened in 1885, is a magnificent, turreted structure with mansard roofs glistening with gold leaf. Commissioned by government authorities, the building combines medieval Gothic, Renaissance, and Baroque motifs with modern iron and glass construction techniques. When Cuypers' design was first revealed, it shocked Calvinist Holland, and Cuypers agreed to tone down some of the more extravagant elements. However, during construction, he visited the site and managed to reinstate many of his original designs. Cuypers' daring architecture created

an influential national style in the Netherlands. He also revived the art of colored brickwork in Holland by encouraging the manufacture of bricks in brilliant greens, reds, and yellows, and by training workman to use them properly.

The Rijksmuseum was founded in 1808 by the newly–created king of Holland, Louis Napoleon, who decreed that all Dutch masterpieces which had not been taken away to Paris be hung in Amsterdam's Town Hall. He then opened the collection to the public and began to acquire works by living artists. Now the largest museum in the Netherlands, the Rijksmuseum has an unparalleled collection of Dutch painting from the fifteenth to eighteenth centuries, with five rooms alone devoted to the paintings of Rembrandt, including his famous *Night Watch.*

The Musée d'Orsay

A new museum set in an old structure, Paris' Musée d'Orsay opened its doors in 1986. Devoted to mainly French painting, sculpture, and photography of the period 1848 to 1914, an era which encompasses Impressionism, this popular museum is housed under the great iron and glass barrel vault of a former train station, the Gare d'Orsay. When the last train pulled out of the station in 1969, the building, designed by architect Victor Laloux, and built in 1900 by the Paris–Orléans railway company, was used as a theater, then as an auction house and a

BELOW: This spectacular view of the interior of the Musée d'Orsay shows how well a great train station can be converted into a great museum. The former station's iron and glass vault creates a magnificent, light–filled space for the exhibition of artworks.

film set. It was saved from demolition by the Parisian preservationist spirit of the late 1970s, when French President Valéry Giscard d'Estaing spearheaded its transformation and the architects Pierre Colboc, Renaud Bardou, and Jean–Paul Philippon were charged with creating a new national museum. Italian architect Gae Aulenti was hired to remodel the interior, and she has preserved the vast light feeling of the original train shed as well as historic details such as the enormous ornate station clock, coffered ceiling vaults, and period light fixtures. In 1900, the iron and glass vault of the Gare d'Orsay symbolized the peak of technological progress by using a new type of construction which had had a spectacular debut in the Crystal Palace, a London exhibition pavilion of 1850. A century later, this same structure evokes a fond nostalgia for the grandeur and optimism of that period, which began with the European revolutions of 1848 and concluded with the First World War.

THE BOSTON TRADITION

Boston Museum of Fine Arts

Neoclassicism remained a popular style of museum construction well into the first half of the twentieth century. The decorative and structural forms of Greece, Rome, and the Italian Renaissance were now more than ever weighted with the cultural symbolism of the grandeur of western civilization, and commonly used for institutions of education, finance, and government, as well as memorials and emblems of civic pride.

When the Boston Museum of Fine Arts, founded in 1870, had outgrown its two previous buildings, the Boston–born but *Ecole des Beaux–Arts*–trained architect Guy Lowell was hired to design its new quarters. Lowell's Museum has all the elements of a Neoclassical temple of the arts—a porticoed entrance with columns, a grand staircase entrance with a barrel–vaulted ceiling pierced by skylights, a rotunda topped with a Pantheon–like dome, masonry construction, and a centralized plan of galleries enclosing skylit courts.

Opened to the public in 1909, Lowell's spacious plan finally succumbed to the need for expansion, and the elegant new west wing was opened in 1981. Designed by I.M. Pei & Partners, the new wing is connected to the original building and compliments it both by completing the circulation loop for the entire museum and by preserving the Neoclassical spirit of the original structure. Pei used the same granite as in the Lowell building, although the façade is smoothly dressed and unembellished. Visitors entering the west wing are drawn up by escalators into daylight which pours from an open circle in the ceiling, a modern variation on the grand staircase. The core of Pei's building is a 225–foot–long (69–meter) galleria topped with a 52–feet–high (16–meter) glass barrel vault, a modern variation on a classical form used by Lowell. The west wing contains three restaurants, special exhibition galleries, and an auditorium, all important in bringing the museum into its twentieth–century role as a social and cultural center.

RIGHT: The Museum of Fine Arts in Boston is one of many museums built in the Neoclassical style espoused by the *Ecole des Beaux–Arts.* Particularly apt for arts institutions, it is a style that goes back to the roots of Western civilization in the cultures of ancient Greece and Rome.

LEFT: The grand staircase of the Museum of Fine Arts in Boston was first seen by the public in 1909 when the new Neoclassical museum designed by Guy Lowell was opened. The staircase with its classical columns and barrel–vaulted ceiling provides an attractive passage from the world outside to the museum's art–filled galleries.

FOLLOWING PAGE: The façade of the new wing of Boston's Museum of Fine Arts is faced with the same type of stone as the main building, although its surface is plain and unembellished. Designed by I.M. Pei & Partners and opened in 1981, the new wing faithfully captures the spirit of the older building.

The National Gallery of Art

The National Gallery of Art in Washington, D.C., is housed in a massive Neoclassical building (1935–40) designed by Beaux–Arts–trained architect John Russell Pope, and an East Building opened in 1978 and designed by I.M. Pei. Although thoroughly modern, Pei's East Building has a monumental elegance that harmonizes with the Neoclassical character of

BELOW: The National Gallery of Art in Washington, D.C. is home to one of America's finest collections of European art, donated to the nation in the 1930s by Andrew Mellon, who was also largely responsible for building the museum. The National Gallery, which opened in 1940, is the work of John Russell Pope.

Pope's museum. Pei's façade is clad in smoothly–dressed pink granite from the same quarry in Tennessee which supplied Pope's stone. Challenged with an unusual trapezoidal site, Pei arrived at a design solution that uses the triangle as an essential design element. Exterior walls converge at a sharp angle that critics have compared to the chiseled edge of an iceberg. Pope's building, with its columned portico and grand rotunda, is connected to the East Building at the basement level by a concourse given over to a museum store and restaurant. Pei's building has its own ceremonial space, a huge skylit inner court which creates a feeling of spiritual uplift. Pei's style may be modern, but the intention of his building retains the continuity of spirit sought by earlier museum architects working in the Neoclassical style.

LEFT: The interior of the East Wing of Washington's National Gallery is a vast, open, uncluttered space that is perfect for the exhibition of monumental modern sculptures and such ample works as the mobile by Alexander Calder, seen here.

BELOW: The East Building of the National Gallery was designed by I. M. Pei and opened to the public in 1978. Though seemingly radically different from the Neoclassical main building, it nevertheless sits in harmony with the older structure.

The Tate Gallery

London's Tate Gallery opened in 1897 in a Neoclassical building designed by architect Sidney J. R. Smith. Originally called the National Gallery of British Art, it was built to house the collection of nineteenth–century painting and sculpture donated by Sir Henry Tate. The original building has a Neoclassical façade and a Corinthian portico crowned with a monumental statue of Britannia. The Tate has seen various expansions, notably the Clore Gallery for the famed Turner Collection, designed by architects James Stirling, Michael Wilford and Associates and opened in 1987. It has also opened several domestic satellite branches, the Tate Gallery Liverpool and the Tate Gallery St. Ives, which represent a growing trend for museums to expand into branches—whether within a city, a country, or even internationally—rather than adding wings in this era where original site capacities have already been fully utilized.

ABOVE: One of London's most popular museums, the Tate Gallery, dating from 1897 was built to house a collection of paintings and sculptures that had been donated to the nation by Sir Henry Tate. This Neo-classical structure was designed by Sidney J.R. Smith.

RIGHT: This domed neo–Baroque rotunda welcomes visitors to London's Tate Gallery. Like the Guggenheim Museum in New York, the Tate has not only expanded its existing premises, but has opened several branch museums around Britain.

CHAPTER THREE

TWENTIETH—CENTURY INNOVATIONS

The International style, which first emerged in Europe and America during the 1920s and '30s, stresses the logic of form following function. The expression of structure as volume rather than mass, the enclosure of a dynamic space, and the lightening of mass are key elements.

The Museum of Modern Art

Museum design entered the twentieth century with a plan by American architects Philip L. Goodwin and Edward Durell Stone for the Museum of Modern Art in New York. Opened in 1939, MoMA was among the earliest examples of International style used for a public building in the United States. A few years after the museum's founding by wealthy art patrons Abby Aldrich Rockefeller, Lillie P. Bliss, and Mary Sullivan, an architectural exhibition at the young but ambitious institution defined International style to the public for the first time.

The new building's design, intended to serve as a symbol of modern art, was a radical departure from tradition. The museum presented a flat, unadorned façade of marble veneer, tile, and opaque and transparent glass. The interior design was shaped by flexible galleries, non–loadbearing walls, and movable partitions that could easily accommodate changing exhibitions—an innovation soon to become standard practice

ABOVE: Manhattan's Museum of Modern Art has lived up to its name by defining Modernism for the twentieth century. Built in 1939 by architects Philip L. Goodwin and Edward Durell Stone, the building was expanded and altered in 1984 under the guidance of Cesar Pelli & Associates.

LEFT: The entry way into the Guggenheim Museum, as in many Wright buildings, is low and unimpressive. From this rather small and dark doorway, the visitor emerges into the light of the rotunda and can see the entire museum, with its swirling spiral ramp and glass dome, at a glance.

LEFT: Unlike some museums, the scale of the Museum of Modern Art's galleries do not overwhelm. Instead, they provide an intimate space for viewing the works of artists who do not always work on a large scale. The innovative use of neutral white walls is also key to the appreciation of many modern paintings.

in many museums. Another widely–copied innovation was the neutral environment of white walls used to display art. The domestic scale of the galleries lent an intimacy to the viewing of the outstanding collection of modern painting, sculpture, photography, film, and industrial design.

In 1984, an alteration and expansion by the architects Cesar Pelli & Associates doubled MoMA'S exhibition space. The original white façade is now set like a jewel of modernism between façades covered with panels of opaque gray glass. A four–story, glass–enclosed garden hall, complete with escalators and a view of architect Philip Johnson's delightful sculpture garden, provides a dramatic public space. In 1997, Japanese architect

Yoshio Taniguchi was chosen to design a further expansion, which will conform to the International–style character of midtown Manhattan.

The Solomon R. Guggenheim Museum

Museum architecture took a different direction in 1943 when collector Solomon R. Guggenheim commissioned architect Frank Lloyd Wright to design a unique building to hold his avant–garde art collection. Wright did not live to see his creation, for construction was completed in 1959 six months after his death. However, the museum is testimony to Wright's creativity and utopian vision—the building is both a work of art and a museum space which functions as a temple for the spirit.

Envisioning a building that would break the rectilinear grid of New York City and also shatter existing ideas about museums, Wright chose the circle as a planning tool and formal element in his museum. The result is a six–story concrete spiral enclosing a rotunda the full height of the building, overlooked by the balconies of a gently–sloping continuous ramp, and topped by a skylit dome. Curiously, though radical in form, the round, top–lit shape of the Guggenheim harks back to the Tribune of the Uffizi, as well as the Pantheon–like ceremonial spaces of many previous museums. Critics of the Guggenheim contend that the bays in which the paintings are hung limit the flexibility of display, and the slope of the ramp interferes with viewing. However, the open balconies of the spiral ramp also

ABOVE: For years one of the most beloved art destinations in New York has been the Sculpture Garden of the Museum of Modern Art. Designed by Philip Johnson, it is an oasis of serenity in the heart of midtown Manhattan.

RIGHT: This view of the interior of the Museum of Modern Art, captured from the outside at dusk, reveals three floors of galleries alive with a swarm of art lovers enjoying one the museum's influential retrospective exhibitions.

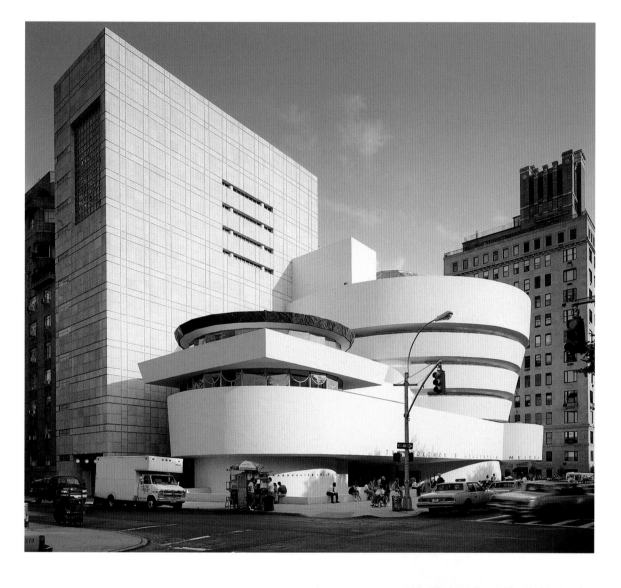

LEFT: The Solomon R. Guggenheim Museum on New York's Fifth Avenue. To the right is the original, revolutionary structure designed by Frank Lloyd Wright and opened in 1959. To the left is the much–needed 1993 addition to the building by Gwathmey Siegel & Associates.

allow the viewing of art from a distance across the rotunda space. This relatively intimate scale also makes the ramps ideal for people watching, and underscores the growing role of the modern museum as a meeting place and social center.

A 1993 addition and restoration by Gwathmey Siegel & Associates Architects successfully sets off the spiral of Wright's landmark building against the geometric counterpoint of an International–style structure, while providing much needed additional space for an expanding collection. This truly inter-national museum—which began as the "Museum of Non–Objective Painting" housing a collection of early abstract works, including many by the Russian painter Wassily Kandinsky—has become a world–famous collection of mod-ern art with branches in New York's Soho district, and abroad, in Italy, Spain, and Germany. The Guggenheim is also design-ing a Virtual Museum for the twenty–first century to create a new architectural paradigm by offering a window into Guggenheim Museums around the world and providing a

ABOVE: The often criticized spiral ramp in Wright's Guggenheim Museum offers features not found in other museums. The viewing space is continuous and open, allowing the visitor not only to see art directly and up–close, but from a distance and at different angles.

unique and compelling spatial environment for the virtual visitor. There, art and events created specifically for the interactive digital medium will be able to be viewed simultaneously by an audience scattered throughout the world.

The Whitney Museum of American Art

In 1966, soon after the opening of the Guggenheim, another New York museum aspiring to be both symbol and sculpture was created by American architect and furniture designer Marcel Breuer. Breuer brought to his design for the Whitney the legacy of his years of study at Germany's famed Bauhaus. Bauhaus style was characterized by economy of method, severe geometry of form, and a concern for the nature of

materials—all functions that played a hand in Breuer's design. The new Whitney building took the form of an inverted ziggurat, with successive levels cantilevered out over each other. The site, in the midst of Madison Avenue's gallery district, underscored the new cultural prominence of American art. The body of the museum is clad in dark gray granite, with the entrance canopy formed of sand–colored concrete. Visitors enter the building by crossing a bridge over a moat that separates the museum physically and psychologically from the surrounding city. Interiors are tall, to accommodate the heroic scale of contemporary American art, and flexible, thanks to a system of moveable partitions. The museum originated from a gallery in the studio of sculptor and collector Gertrude Vanderbilt Whitney. The first museum devoted exclusively to American art, the Whitney opened its doors to the public in 1931.

The Getty Villa

The Neoclassical revival at the beginning of the nineteenth century had been fueled by the classical archaeological discoveries of the eighteenth century. Newly–discovered antiquities from ancient Greek and Roman civilizations were widely publicized through books and engravings, and inspired many artists and architects of the period. The unearthing of the lost cities of Herculaneum and Pompeii in Italy, which had been buried by an eruption of Mount Vesuvius in AD 79, were greeted with great excitement because of the remarkable state of preservation of the buildings, decorations, and furnishings—not to mention the bodies of the inhabitants.

LEFT: The Whitney Museum of American Art, opened in 1966, is the work of Bauhaus–trained architect and furniture designer Marcel Breuer. Designed in the shape of an inverted ziggurat, it is faced with gray granite and separated from the street by a moat.

The Getty Villa in Malibu, California (formerly the J. Paul Getty Museum), is an authentic recreation of a Roman villa uncovered at Herculaneum. Collector J. Paul Getty chose the architectural firm of Langdon & Wilson (designers of the Getty Oil Company building in Los Angeles), to make his dream a reality. The Villa is approached along a garden walkway bordered by a pond and grand colonnade, and entered through bronze doors. Built to house Getty's collection of Greek and Roman antiquities, as well as paintings, the design strove for authenticity in every detail. Getty's Villa mirrors the original floor plan and decorations of Piso's Villa—an interior peristyle and atrium are decorated with stucco; walls are painted in the authentic Pompeian manner; and floors are highlighted with marble and mosaic. Situated in a narrow valley, the Villa faces the Pacific Ocean and offers fine views framed by tall trees. Built in 1974, the Getty Villa is currently being repaired following earthquake damage, and will reopen in 2001.

RIGHT: The Getty Villa in Malibu, California is an authentic reproduction of a Roman villa in Herculaneum that was buried by the same eruption of Mount Vesuvius that also destroyed Pompeii. This aerial view shows the vast extent of this building which houses Greek and Roman artworks.

The Pompidou Center

If the Getty Villa reached back to a pre–museum age by striving to display a collection in its original context, the Pompidou Center in Paris reaches forward to a post–museum age to create a space that is both a flexible container and a dynamic machine for communication. Intended from the beginning as a place that would be attractive and accessible to the widest possible segment of the public, the Center's concept was to be

a living center of information, entertainment, and culture. Architects Richard Rogers and Renzo Piano were chosen to design the Center, which houses an important collection of twentieth–century art, architecture, and design. The vast glass and steel structure rises seven stories on its site next to an open plaza in Paris' Beaubourg neighborhood. To achieve the largest unobstructed interior space, all of the building's systems are on the exterior, from the plastic tube escalators to the electrical, air conditioning, and water systems housed in bright, color–coded pipes. This externalizing of systems is common in industry, but unique in museum architecture, and that lends the Center a gaudy, machine–age character which has made it an extraordinarily popular attraction. Wear and tear, however, has necessitated renovation, and the Center will reopen to the public at the end of 1999.

BELOW: The Pompidou Center, in the Beaubourg district of Paris, is in many ways the world's most unusual museum. To maximize exhibition space, all of the building's systems and necessary equipment were placed on the outside of the structure.

LEFT: The Pompidou Center was designed by architects Richard Rogers and Renzo Piano. It is a glass and steel structure that offers seven stories of exhibition space. Unfortunately, due to its popularity and subsequent wear and tear, it has been closed for renovations. It is scheduled to reopen at the end of 1999.

LEFT: Built to house a collection of twentieth—century art, architecture, and design, the Pompidou Center is one of the most popular artistic attractions in Paris. Its industrial look and non—traditional character are appealing to the younger generation and the wider art audience.

The National Air and Space Museum

Need for vast interior spaces and the capacity to accommodate millions of visitors a year also shaped the architecture of the Smithsonian Institution's National Air and Space Museum in Washington, D. C., which opened in 1976. Gyo Obata of the architectural firm of Hellmuth, Obata and Kassabaum undertook the challenge to create a building that was as big as possible and had a modular structural system strong enough to hang airplanes from, yet was flexible enough to accommodate rockets. The rockets are in a hole in the floor called a missile pit, and airplanes hang from the ceiling, which is 83 feet high (25 meters), 685 feet long (204 meters), 225 feet wide (69 meters), and divided into seven bays. Four marble boxes are connected to three glass bays; the bays are topped by skylights and serve as dramatic, full–height exhibition areas. The unadorned marble façade is a curtain wall hung on steel, and exposed steel trusses span the glass–enclosed bays to support the airplanes. The building houses a planetarium, an auditorium, and 200,000 square feet (60,600 meters) of exhibition space and themed exhibits including everything from the first Wright Brothers plane of 1903 to the Apollo II command module and a piece of moon rock that can be touched.

RIGHT: The Smithsonian Institution's National Air and Space Museum in Washington, D.C. is one of the capital's most popular attractions. Historic vintage airplanes, including Linbergh's *Spirit of Saint Louis*, hang from the ceiling and can be compared and admired by both aviation and history buffs alike.

LEFT: One of the most fascinating exhibits at the National Air and Space Museum is the lunar landing vehicle that played such a pivotal role in the Apollo moon missions. Similar offerings include rockets installed in missile pits.

FOLLOWING PAGE: No matter what one's views of Wright's museum might be, a trip to the Guggenheim is never dull. The building itself is a tour de force, whether viewed from the floor looking up, or from the top downward.

The San Francisco Museum of Modern Art

Opened in January 1995, the San Francisco Museum of Modern Art quickly fulfilled its mission as a unique, instantly recognizable structure that symbolically proclaims its importance. Swiss architect Mario Botta produced a building that stands out from the city in form, style, and materials. A massive, windowless volume steps back from the street in deep tiers, crowned by the black–and–white striped cylindrical turret of its skylight. The top of the cylinder is cut off at an angle, causing the ellipse of the skylight to resemble a circular *oculus,* or eye, a symbol entirely appropriate for a museum of visual arts. The pre–cast structure is clad in bands of rusticated red brick accented with black and white granite. Curiously, the

fortress–like impression evaporates on entering the soaring interior space of the central rotunda. Facing the entrance, the dramatic central staircase of black granite and lobby appointments of maple give an impression of corporate wealth. The central rotunda and grand stair also evoke the traditional forms of museum architecture. High above the rotunda, an open–weave steel footbridge allows visitors to cross the sun–drenched, vertiginous space. Galleries are lit by skylights, and a balcony offers a splendid view of the city overlooking the cultural and civic complex of Yerba Buena Gardens. Botta's building gave SFMOMA the instant identity and popularity that had eluded it in the bland Beaux Arts Veterans Building it had occupied since 1935.

ABOVE: Dramatic as it is by day, the San Francisco Museum of Modern Art is even more impressive at night. The lines and colors of the building, including its rusticated red bricks, are strikingly highlighted and lit, creating a new form, nighttime architecture

RIGHT: The San Francisco Museum of Modern Art with its central skylight. The museum, opened in 1995 and designed by Swiss architect Mario Botta, is a massive windowless structure with ascending setbacks in deep tiers from the street.

The Getty Center

Opened in December 1997, the Getty Center, a 110–acre campus of white buildings situated on a hilltop, is an impressive and massive declaration of Los Angeles' cultural preeminence. Architect Richard Meier was chosen to design the billion–dollar project, which he considers an ideal version of social space. The Getty Center aims to provide visitors not only with a museum experience, but also with the opportunity to enjoy a relaxing outdoor setting, with terraces, balconies, gardens, water features, and views of the city from the mountains to the sea. This elegant late modern complex is unified by its deeply–textured travertine, and isolated from the city by its hilltop site in Brentwood. Visitors must park at the bottom and ride a high–tech tram to the Center, which houses all the branches of the J. Paul Getty Trust. In a bow to tradition, the pavilions of the J. Paul Getty Museum are approached by a grand staircase, and entered through a soaring rotunda hall. Traditionally displayed collections highlight pre–twentieth–century European paintings, drawings, sculpture, manuscripts, and decorative arts.

ABOVE: Billionaire J. Paul Getty left most of his vast fortune to a museum to be established in his name in California. For many years now, the museum's expansion projects in both building and in the acquisition of art have been enormous. This aerial view shows the Getty as it is today.

ABOVE: Completely unlike museums of the past and truly a museum of the twenty–first century, the Getty Center with its vast resources has become a Southern California tourist mecca. Only its placement in a seismic region causes concern. However, the public has been assured that all efforts have been made to protect the collection from earthquake damage.

LEFT: Unlike most museums, the Getty Center is not located in the heart of a bustling city. Instead, it is sited in pleasant countryside where the museum–goer can experience expansive views, the outdoors, and quiet spots for relaxation and refreshment, as well as the museum's impressive collection.

The Guggenheim Museum Bilbao

The new Guggenheim Museum Bilbao is a sculptural work of art, an architectural landmark, and a unique and instantly famous symbol created by architect Frank Gehry for one of Spain's culturally ambitious cities. Opened in 1997, the Guggenheim Bilbao is crowned by the twisting, curving shapes of a titanium–clad roof, nicknamed the "metallic flower." The fluid complex shapes were made possible by a computer program known as Catia, which allows sculptural explorations while maintaining control of practical construction. Interconnected limestone units house galleries, an auditorium, a restaurant, a store, and administrative offices, unified by the metal roof covered with a thin skin of titanium, a metal similar in color and reflectivity to stainless steel. A 165–foot–high (50–meter) light–flooded atrium, its grandeur alluding to cathedral architecture, is a central feature. The Guggenheim Bilbao's rhythmic quality is enhanced by elaborate bridges, stairways, catwalks, and glass elevators offering glimpses of sky and the nearby Nervi) light–flooded atrium, its grandeur alluding to cathedral architecture, is a central feature. The Guggenheim Bilbao's rhythmic quality is enhanced by elaborate bridges, stairways, catwalks, and glass elevators offering glimpses of sky agalleries accommodate more traditional art.

The Miho Museum

I.M. Pei's singular creativity is exemplified in the Miho Museum, built on a mountain top in a nature preserve near Kyoto. Opened in November 1997, the Miho was built by the Japanese religious organization Shinji Shumeikai to house an exquisite collection of Japanese and ancient art assembled by its founders—Mihoko and Hiroko Koyama. The two women worked with Pei to fulfill their dream of a museum that would embody their belief that spiritual fulfillment can be attained through beauty in art and nature.

In Japan, only temples are traditionally built on mountains peaks, as mountains are considered sacred. Pei's museum preserves the sacred and contemplative experience through

ABOVE: The entrance to the Guggenheim Museum Bilbao leads to an array of galleries that range in size from spaces for displaying giant artworks to traditionally proportioned rooms for more conservative art.

traditional temple forms, such as the slanting silhouettes of the glass and steel rooftops, and the harmonizing of the museum with its natural setting. This was achieved by keeping the buildings under 40 feet high (12 meters), and limiting the amount of the limestone clad building that is visible. The top of the mountain was literally removed, the museum built, and the earth returned to cover the buildings so that ninety–five percent of the structure is below ground. The approach to the museum requires a literal and spiritual journey through a tunnel, across a unique suspension bridge, and up a stairway lined with stone lanterns, through a moon–shaped door and into a light–filled atrium hall, where views of the neighboring valley, temple, and bell tower are framed by carefully selected trees. The Miho's mission—to create an environment of contemplation and tranquillity in which to appreciate art objects of exceptional value and beauty—is remarkably similar to the intent of the earliest museums such as the Uffizi's Tribune. Some of the Miho's galleries, in fact, evoke the traditional Tribune form of polygonal sides and natural top lighting that

have shaped museum design—and ideas about art display—from the Renaissance to the end of the twentieth century.

Working Towards the Future

The original aims of museums—to preserve, to educate, and to uplift—are still current today. Likewise, the idea of the museum building as a symbol of a city or country's cultural prestige, exists today with the same force as 200 or more years ago. The last fifty years have seen the evolution of museums into social centers and meeting places; the Internet has the ability to remove the museum experience from architecture entirely.

Tracing the development of museums from personal treasure–troves to multi–functioned cultural institutions offers a fascinating journey through time. The history of museum architecture has been shaped by the fluctuations of power, wealth, and taste of many nations, and the visions of many individual architects. The continuing evolution of museums can draw on both the rich traditions of the past and contemporary innovations to shape the future.

ABOVE: The immediate success of the Guggenheim Museum Bilbao has been overwhelming. Designed by architect Frank Gehry and opened in 1997, it is distinguished by the undulating shapes of its roof, which have given it the nickname "metallic flower."